My Cousin Is in the
NATIONAL GUARD

JIM THOMPSON

New York

Published in 2016 by The Rosen Publishing Group, Inc.
29 East 21st Street, New York, NY 10010

First Edition

Editor: Sarah Machajewski
Book Design: Katelyn Heinle/Reann Nye

Photo Credits: Cover, pp. 5 (soldier), 22 Tim Bieber/Digital Vision/Getty Images; cover backdrop, p. 1 David Smart/Shutterstock.com; pp. 3–4, 6, 8, 10, 12, 14, 16, 18, 20, 22, 24 (camouflage texture) Casper1774/Shutterstock.com; pp. 7 (top), 9 (both), 15 (bottom), 17 (both), 21 courtesy of U.S. National Guard Flickr; p. 7 (bottom) Burlingham/Shutterstock.com; p. 11 (top) Joe Raedle/Getty Images News/Getty Images; p. 11 (bottom) Wesley Bocxe/Science Source/Getty Images; p. 13 Spencer Platt/ Getty Images News/Getty Images; p. 15 (map) ekler/Shutterstock.com; p. 19 John Tlumacki/The Boston Globe/Getty Images; p. 22 (flag background) Naypong/Shutterstock.com.

Library of Congress Cataloging-in-Publication Data

Names: Thompson, Jim, 1979-
Title: My cousin is in the National Guard / Jim Thompson.
Description: New York : PowerKids Press, [2016] | Series: Military families | Includes index.
Identifiers: LCCN 2015036307 | ISBN 9781508144588 (pbk.) | ISBN 9781508144472 (6 pack) | ISBN 9781508144489 (library bound)
Subjects: LCSH: United States-National Guard-Juvenile literature.
Classification: LCC UA42 .T49 2016 | DDC 355.3/70973-dc23
LC record available at http://lccn.loc.gov/2015036307

Manufactured in the United States of America

CPSIA Compliance Information: Batch #BW16PK: For Further Information contact Rosen Publishing, New York, New York at 1-800-237-9932

CONTENTS

Meet My Cousin

The United States has one of the biggest and most powerful militaries in the world. More than 2 million men and women have **dedicated** their lives to serving our country and its citizens. One of those people is my cousin. He's in the National Guard.

My cousin joined the military because he wanted to serve his country. Joining the military is a big decision, or choice. It can change a person's life—and their family members' lives, too. I learned a lot about the National Guard after my cousin joined. Let me tell you about it!

I'M PROUD OF MY COUSIN FOR SERVING IN THE NATIONAL GUARD.

PART OF THE MILITARY

When people decide to join the military, they can join one of five branches. The five branches are the army, air force, navy, Marine **Corps**, and coast guard. The National Guard is part of the army and the air force.

These branches have an active-duty force, which is made of people who serve full time. They also have reserve forces, which are made of people who serve part time. The National Guard is a reserve force. There is an Army National Guard and an Air National Guard. My cousin is a soldier in the Army National Guard.

★ ★ ★
MILITARY MATTERS
People who serve in the National Guard are sometimes called "citizen-soldiers."

ACTIVE-DUTY
SOLDIER

NATIONAL GUARD
SOLDIER

CITIZEN-SOLDIERS DON'T WORK FOR THE MILITARY FULL TIME. MANY HAVE OTHER JOBS IN ADDITION TO SERVING IN THE NATIONAL GUARD. THEY SERVE WHEN THE MILITARY NEEDS THEM.

Forming the National Guard

The Army National Guard can trace its history back to the 1600s, before the United States was a country. The first militias formed after Jamestown Colony was settled in 1607. A militia is a group of citizens who come together to fight in times of need. Other colonies formed their own militias later.

After the United States became an independent country, states were allowed to have their own militia forces. By 1903, state militias were known as the "national guard." Today, this is the official name for this important reserve force.

★★★
Military Matters
As of 2015, the Army National Guard has more than 350,000 soldiers.

1913

2015

MY COUSIN IS PROUD TO BE PART OF ONE OF THE UNITED STATES' OLDEST MILITARY ORGANIZATIONS.

What Does the National Guard Do?

The Army National Guard is part of the U.S. Army, which means it's under the control of the federal government. However, the National Guard is special because it's also under the control of a state's government. Both the federal government and state governments can call on the National Guard when they need it.

My cousin has a lot to do as a National Guard soldier. Soldiers **protect** the United States at home and overseas. They serve during times of **crisis**, such as when hurricanes, floods, and earthquakes occur. National Guard soldiers have served in **combat**, carried out laws, and helped keep order during **protests** and other events.

MORE THAN 50,000 NATIONAL GUARD SOLDIERS TRAVELED TO NEW ORLEANS, LOUISIANA, AND SURROUNDING STATES AFTER HURRICANE KATRINA IN 2005.

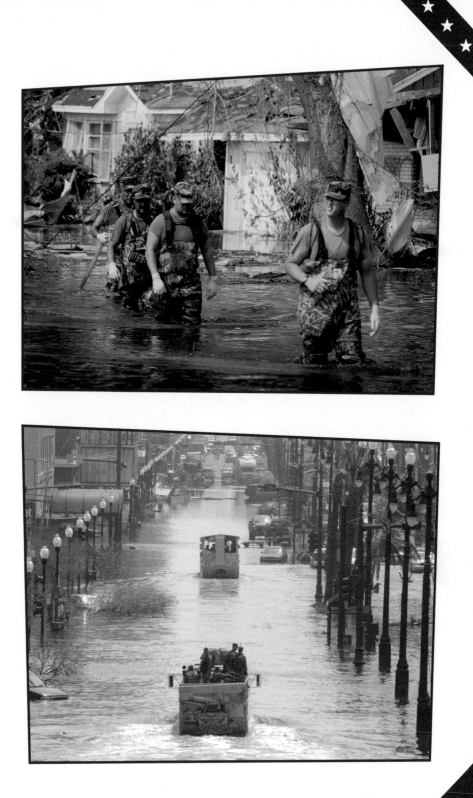

How to Join

My cousin had to meet some requirements to join the National Guard. **Recruits** have to be between 17 and 35 years old. They must be citizens, but people who have lawfully entered the United States can join, too. Recruits also must have a high school **diploma** or a GED, which is something much like a high school diploma.

My cousin had to take a test called the ASVAB before he could join the National Guard. The ASVAB asks questions about reading, math, science, electronics, and putting together objects. It helps future soldiers figure out what their job with the National Guard will be.

MY COUSIN LEARNED ABOUT JOINING THE NATIONAL
GUARD FROM A RECRUITER. A RECRUITER IS A SOLDIER
WHO HELPS PEOPLE JOIN THE MILITARY. THEY CAN ANSWER
QUESTIONS ABOUT WHAT IT'S LIKE TO SERVE IN THE NATIONAL
GUARD, WHAT SOLDIERS' LIVES ARE LIKE, AND HOW SERVING
AFFECTS THEIR FAMILIES.

OFF TO TRAINING

Basic combat training (BCT) is the first thing recruits do after **enlisting** in the military. It lasts 10 weeks. National Guard recruits train with the rest of the army.

During boot camp, recruits learn how to be a soldier. They learn to be strong and prepared for anything. They also learn how to use **weapons** and how to work as a team.

Basic training can be hard for recruits because they have to leave home. We weren't able to talk to my cousin while he was at training. We were able to write him letters, though. I missed him a lot.

★★★
MILITARY MATTERS
Basic training is also called boot camp.

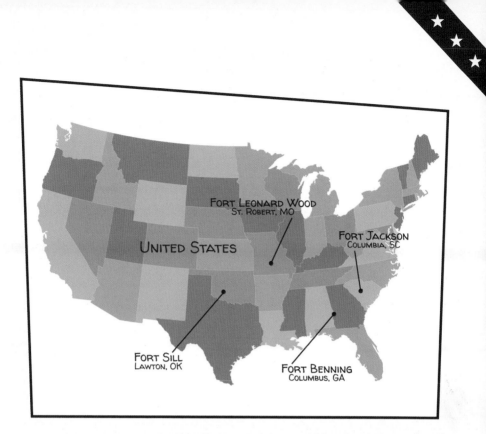

FORT LEONARD WOOD
ST. ROBERT, MO

FORT JACKSON
COLUMBIA, SC

UNITED STATES

FORT SILL
LAWTON, OK

FORT BENNING
COLUMBUS, GA

THE ARMY HAS FOUR PLACES FOR BASIC TRAINING. THEY'RE FORT BENNING IN GEORGIA, FORT JACKSON IN SOUTH CAROLINA, FORT LEONARD WOOD IN MISSOURI, AND FORT SILL IN OKLAHOMA.

TRAINING FOR THE JOB

After 10 weeks, my cousin graduated from training. He was finally a citizen-soldier, but his training wasn't done. He soon left for Advanced Individual Training (AIT). During AIT, he trained for his job in the army. This is known as a Military Occupational Specialty, or MOS.

My cousin's MOS is as a cargo specialist. He helps transport, or move, supplies and support to army forces. He makes sure the army's weapons, **equipment**, and mail get where they need to go. This is just one career the National Guard offers. Many soldiers say their job in the National Guard helps them in their other job, too.

THE NATIONAL GUARD HAS MILITARY POLICE, MECHANICS, DOCTORS, AND MORE. THERE ARE MORE THAN 150 CAREERS TO CHOOSE FROM.

My Cousin's Life

My cousin likes being in the National Guard. He trains once a month at a training center nearby. He attends annual training for two weeks a year. Training is also called "drill." When he isn't training, he works at his other job and spends time with my family.

Even though my cousin isn't a full-time soldier, he must always be ready to serve. There's always a chance our state will need him to help with something important. The federal government may need him, too. He stays healthy and practices his skills so he's always ready.

IF A DISASTER HAPPENS, THE NATIONAL GUARD IS READY TO HELP. IN 2015, A HUGE SNOWSTORM HIT BOSTON, MASSACHUSETTS. THE NATIONAL GUARD, INCLUDING MY COUSIN, TRAVELED THERE TO HELP REMOVE THE SNOW.

A Military Family

My family's life changed a little after my cousin joined the National Guard, but some parts have stayed the same. Active-duty soldiers have to live on an **army base**, but reserve soldiers can live near their families. It's nice having my cousin so close by.

My family knows my cousin can be called on at any time to serve. National Guard soldiers can be sent overseas, and they can see combat. Some **missions** they help with can be dangerous, or unsafe. This is scary for my family, but we support my cousin. We're really proud of what he does!

ONE OF THE MOST IMPORTANT THINGS FAMILIES CAN DO IS SUPPORT THEIR SOLDIER AND OUR MILITARY. IT MAKES SOLDIERS FEEL BETTER TO KNOW PEOPLE ARE STANDING BEHIND THEM.

OUR COUNTRY'S HEROES

Having a family member in the military is very special. However, it's not always easy. It can be hard to say good-bye to your family member when they leave for training or if they're sent away from home. When my cousin goes away to serve or train, I miss him. But I feel better when I talk to my family about how I feel.

I look up to my cousin a lot. I'm proud he chose to serve in the National Guard. Our military's servicemen and servicewomen do a lot for our country. They're my heroes!

Glossary

army base: A place owned and operated by the army where soldiers train and equipment is held.

combat: Fighting between armed forces.

corps: A group within a branch of a military organization that does a particular kind of work.

crisis: A time of difficulty, trouble, or danger.

dedicate: To give yourself to a certain task or purpose.

diploma: A piece of paper that shows somebody has finished a certain level of schooling.

enlist: To join.

equipment: The objects needed for a certain purpose.

mission: An important job.

protect: To keep safe.

protest: An event when people come together to show they don't agree with something.

recruit: A person new to the armed forces who is not yet fully trained.

weapon: Something used to cause harm.

Index

Websites

Due to the changing nature of Internet links, PowerKids Press has developed an online list of websites related to the subject of this book. This site is updated regularly. Please use this link to access the list: www.powerkidslinks.com/mili/natl